tica

Raintree

Raintree is an imprint of Capstone Global Library Limited, a company incorporated in England and Wales having its registered office at 7 Pilgrim Street, London, EC4V 6LB – Registered company number: 6695582

www.raintreepublishers.co.uk
myorders@raintreepublishers.co.uk

Text © Capstone Global Library Limited 2014
First published in hardback in 2014
Paperback edition first published in 2015
The moral rights of the proprietor have been asserted.

Edited by Dan Nunn, Rebecca Rissman, Sian Smith, and Helen Cox Cannons
Designed by Philippa Jenkins
Original illustrations © Capstone Global Library Ltd 2014
Picture research by Liz Alexander and Tristan Leverett
Production by Vicki Fitzgerald
Originated by Capstone Global Library Ltd
Printed and bound in China by Leo Paper Products Ltd

ISBN 978 1 406 26294 0 (hardback)
17 16 15 14 13
10 9 8 7 6 5 4 3 2 1

ISBN 978 1 406 26303 9 (paperback)
18 17 16 15 14
10 9 8 7 6 5 4 3 2 1

British Library Cataloguing in Publication Data
Ganeri, Anita
Introducing Antarctica – (Introducing continents)
A full catalogue record for this book is available from the British Library.

Acknowledgements
We would like to thank the following for permission to reproduce photographs: Alamy p. 27 (© Images & Stories); Corbis p. 24 (© Robert Weight; Ecoscene); Getty Images pp. 7 (National Geographic /Maria Stenzel), 9 (National Geographic / Gordon Wiltsie), 15 (Kim Westerskov/Stone), 16 (Joseph Van Os/The Image Bank), 17 (The Image Bank/ Doug Allan), 21 (National Geographic/Maria Stenzel); Photoshot pp. 14 (© TTL), 23 (© Eye Ubiquitous); Science Photo Library pp. 6 (John Beatty); Science Photo Library pp. 13 (Canadian Space Agency/Radarsat/NASA), 22 (Karim Agabi/ EURELIOS); Shutterstock pp. 8 (© BMJ), 10 (© Volodymyr Goinyk), 11 (© damerau), 19 (© gary yim), 20 (© spirit of America); SuperStock pp. 12 (Minden Pictures), 18 (Wolfgang Kaehler), 25 (Robert Harding Picture Library), 26 (Universal Images Group).

Cover photographs of a luminescent iceberg in Antarctica and a shaded relief map of Antarctica reproduced with permission of Shutterstock (© Achim Baque, © AridOcean); image of guests from the Lindblad Expedition ship the National Geographic Explorer enjoying Antarctica reproduced with permission of SuperStock (© Michael S. Nolan/age footstock).

Disclaimer
All the internet addresses (URLs) given in this book were valid at the time of going to press. However, due to the dynamic nature of the internet, some addresses may have changed, or sites may have changed or ceased to exist since publication. While the author and publisher regret any inconvenience this may cause readers, no responsibility for any such changes can be accepted by either the author or the publisher.

Contents

Some words are shown in bold, **like this**. You can find out what they mean by looking in the glossary.

About Antarctica

A **continent** is a huge area of land. There are seven continents on Earth. This book is about the continent of Antarctica. Antarctica is the fifth biggest continent.

ARCTIC OCEAN

North America

Europe

Asia

ATLANTIC OCEAN

Africa

PACIFIC OCEAN

Equator

PACIFIC OCEAN

South America

INDIAN OCEAN

Australia

SOUTHERN OCEAN

Antarctica

Antarctica lies at the southern end of the world. It is covered in thick ice and surrounded by the Southern Ocean. In winter, parts of the ocean freeze over.

Antarctica fact file	
Area	14,200,000 square kilometres (5,500,000 square miles)
Population	up to 4,500 visiting scientists
Number of countries	0
Highest mountain	Vinson Massif at 4,897 metres (16,067 feet)
Largest lake	Lake Vostok at 15,690 square kilometres (6,057 square miles)

Famous places

The **South Pole** is the most famous place in Antarctica. It marks the southern end of Earth. A sign shows the position of the Pole. Nearby is a US **research station**.

the South Pole

The small striped pole shows the position of the South Pole.

Mount Erebus is the most southern volcano in the world.

Mount Erebus is a mountain on Ross Island in the Ross Sea. It is 3,794 metres (12,447 feet) high. Mount Erebus is an **active volcano**. It often erupts, shooting out rocks and steam.

Weather

Antarctica is the coldest place on Earth. In winter, the temperature at the **South Pole** is around −60 degrees Celsius (−76 degrees Fahrenheit). The coldest temperature ever recorded was −89.2 degrees Celsius (−128.5 degrees Fahrenheit) at Vostok **research station**.

Antarctica is the coldest and windiest place on Earth.

These scientists are battling against a blizzard in Antarctica.

Antarctica is also the windiest place in the world. There are often storms, called **blizzards**. Blizzards happen when the wind blasts the snow along. The blowing snow makes it difficult to move or see.

Geography

Most of Antarctica is covered in a gigantic sheet of ice. In some places, the ice is 5 kilometres (3 miles) thick. **Glaciers** flow very slowly from the ice sheet into the sea.

This glacier is flowing from the mountains towards the sea.

glacier

Icebergs drift on the Southern Ocean around Antarctica.

Around Antarctica, huge shelves of ice hang over the sea. Sometimes, chunks of ice break off these ice shelves. They float in the sea as **icebergs**. Icebergs also break off glaciers.

The Transantarctic Mountains run right across Antarctica. The tops of the mountains stick up above the ice. Vinson Massif is in the Ellsworth Mountains. It is the highest mountain in Antarctica.

Vinson Massif is 4,897 metres (16,067 feet) tall.

Ellsworth Mountains

Greater Antarctica

Vinson Massif

Transantarctic Mountains

Lesser Antarctica

Mount Erebus

| 0 | 770 miles |
| 0 | 1240 km |

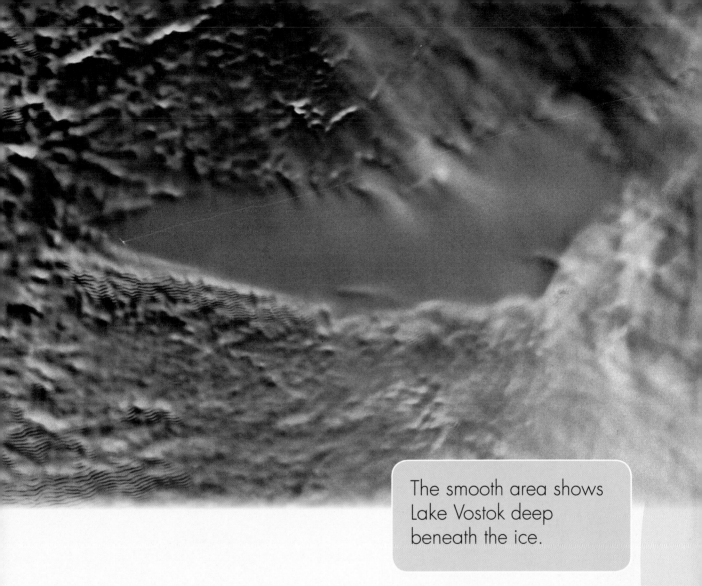

The smooth area shows Lake Vostok deep beneath the ice.

Many large lakes are buried under the ice. Lake Vostok is buried under ice that is about 4 kilometres (2½ miles) thick. The water in the lake is still liquid. It is millions of years old.

Southern Ocean

Antarctica is surrounded by the Southern Ocean. The ocean is very cold and stormy. Strong winds whip the water up into huge waves. There are also smaller seas around the coast.

SOUTHERN OCEAN

SOUTHERN OCEAN

SOUTHERN OCEAN

SOUTHERN OCEAN

| 0 | 770 miles |
| 0 | 1,240 km |

Sailing the stormy Southern Ocean is difficult and dangerous.

An icebreaker is a ship designed for breaking through the frozen ocean.

In winter, parts of the Southern Ocean freeze over. The extra ice makes the **continent** of Antarctica almost twice as big as before. In summer, the ice melts again.

Animals

Despite the cold and wind, some animals live in Antarctica. Emperor penguins **breed** on the ice in the middle of winter. Penguins have a thick layer of fat under their skin. The fat keeps them warm.

These Emperor penguins are walking with their chicks on the Antarctic ice.

Weddell seals have large eyes for seeing in the dark water.

Whales and seals live in the Southern Ocean. Weddell seals live under the sea ice. They eat fish and squid. They chew holes in the ice so that they can reach the surface to breathe.

Other living things

Plants have to be very tough to survive in Antarctica. Lichens are tiny living things that can grow on bare rock. Lichens grow very slowly and can live for thousands of years.

Hardy lichens and moss grow on rocks in Antarctica.

Snow algae in Antarctica can turn whole snowfields red.

Living things, called algae, grow on the snow. They colour large patches of the snow pinkish-red. Their red colouring works like suncream. It stops them getting damaged by the strong sunshine.

Natural resources

Each year, thousands of tourists visit Antarctica. They go to see the beautiful scenery and amazing wildlife. The tourists have to follow strict rules, such as not leaving litter behind or disturbing the animals.

Tourists to Antarctica travel in small boats to see the **icebergs**.

This coal was found under the ice in Antarctica.

Antarctica has many natural resources, such as coal, oil, and **minerals**. These lie deep under the ice. People are not allowed to **mine** or drill for them in case they damage Antarctica.

Countries and people

Antarctica is the only **continent** that does not have its own countries. Today, people from 29 other countries work together to study and look after Antarctica. They include the United Kingdom, the United States, Russia, and Australia.

This **research station** is run jointly by Italy and France.

Scientists send up balloons and equipment to study the weather.

Nobody lives in Antarctica all the time. But each year, thousands of scientists visit Antarctica for a few months. They study the ice, rocks, weather, animals, and plants.

Research stations

The scientists live and work in **research stations**. These are buildings with **living quarters**, **laboratories**, offices, garages, and workshops. Many other people, such as cooks and doctors, also live there.

In summer, about 70 people live at the UK's Halley research station.

Scientists' tents are pyramid shaped, to help them stand up to the wind.

Scientists also spend time away from base. They camp in small tents on the ice or in the mountains. Sometimes, bad weather can trap them inside their tents for days.

Explorers

The first person to reach the **South Pole** was Roald Amundsen from Norway in 1911. He used dogs to pull his sledges. He wore clothes made from wolfskin to keep him warm.

Roald Amundsen put up the Norwegian flag at the South Pole.

These climbers are exploring Vinson Massif, the highest mountain in Antarctica.

People are still exploring Antarctica. They have to train hard and be fit and healthy. They have radios and use **satellites** to help them keep in touch and find their way.

Fun facts

- Antarctica is twice the size of Australia and one and a half times the size of the United States.

- The ice over Antarctica is so heavy that the land has sunk under its weight.

- In Antarctica in winter, it is almost always dark; in summer, it is light most of the time.

- The Lambert **Glacier** in Antarctica is the biggest glacier in the world.

Quiz

1. Who was the first person to reach the **South Pole**?

2. Which animals **breed** on the ice in winter?

3. Which lake is buried underneath the ice?

4. How many people live on Antarctica all of the time?

4. None

3. Vostok

2. Penguins

1. Roald Amundsen

Glossary

active volcano mountain with a hole in the top which ash or hot melted rock comes out of

blizzard storms with strong winds which blow the snow along

breed to have babies

continent one of seven huge areas of land on Earth

glacier very large piece of slow-moving ice

icebergs big chunks of ice that break off glaciers and ice sheets

laboratories places where scientists work

living quarters places where scientists live

mine dig up from under the ground

minerals materials found under the ground

research station place where scientists live and work in Antarctica

satellites objects in space that can help people to find their way

South Pole the most southern place on Earth

Find out more

Books

Antarctica (Exploring Continents), Tristan Boyer Binns (Heinemann Library, 2008)

Oxford First Atlas (OUP, 2010)

Perishing Poles, Anita Ganeri (Scholastic, 2009)

Websites to visit

kids.discovery.com/tell-me/people-and-places/our-7-continents
Games, puzzles, and activities about the seven continents can be found on this website.

kids.nationalgeographic.com/kids/games/geographygames/copycat
This fun game helps you to find the continents on a map of the world.

www.worldatlas.com
This site has lots of maps, facts, and figures about continents.

Index